The *Heyday* of the
BRISTOL RE

Kevin Lane

Ian Allan
PUBLISHING

Front cover: The largest fleet of Bristol REs in mainland Britain was run by United Automobile Services. One of a minority with dual-door bodywork, RELL6G/ECW 5026 (FHN 926J) works a local service in Scarborough on 22 August 1978. *Charles Dean / Author's collection*

Back cover: In Scotland the Bristol RE was a comparatively rare beast. Representing the largest fleet north of the border is Scottish Omnibuses RELH6G/Alexander Y-type ZA184 (EWS 184D), seen on private-hire duties in Kilmarnock in October 1972. *Charles Dean / Author's collection*

Previous page: Recently repainted in NBC poppy red, having been new in the Tilling-green livery still worn by most other buses in the picture, Hants & Dorset Bristol RELL6G/ECW 1606 (NLJ 821G) rests between duties in the old Bournemouth bus station on 9 August 1974. On the left, in Tilling red, is 632 (CRU 142L), one of a final batch of six REs ordered for the Wilts & Dorset fleet but delivered direct to Hants & Dorset in the autumn of 1972. *Mike Greenwood*

Right: Author's favourite! Luton & District Bristol RELH6L/Plaxton 220 (SBD 220M) loads in the High Street in Leighton Buzzard before heading for Luton via Stanbridge and Dunstable in April 1987. The Volvos and Scanias in use today somehow don't have the same appeal... *Author*

First published 2008

ISBN (10) 0 7110 3276 9
ISBN (13) 978 0 7110 3276 7

© Ian Allan Publishing 2008

Published by Ian Allan Publishing
an imprint of Ian Allan Publishing Ltd, Hersham, Surrey, KT12 4RG

Printed in England by Ian Allan Publishing Ltd, Hersham, Surrey, KT12 4RG

Code: 0808/B

Visit the Ian Allan Publishing website at www.ianallanpublishing.com

Introduction

In 1993 *Classic Bus* magazine conducted a survey to find its readers' top 10 favourite buses. The winner was, predictably, a double-decker, and, more predictably, this turned out to be the Routemaster. However, the highest-placed single-decker, at number four, was the Bristol RE. Furthermore, in a later survey to find out which die-cast models the manufacturers should be producing, out on top came the Bristol RE, preferably in ECW bus-bodied form, with curved screen (which was subsequently accomplished). Now, I could have told you all this, having been a fan for many years, and the opportunity to compile this book was most welcome.

It was only towards the end of the 1970s that I became interested in buses, and it seemed to me then that the Bristol RE could be encountered almost everywhere … well, everywhere I went at that time, generally on railway trips (now Crewe … that was a good place for REs!). The Scottish Motorway coaches seemed to me the most exotic and were often to be found after dark loading up at Victoria Coach Station. In contrast (and, initially, a surprise that they should have come from the same stable) were the clattering bus-bodied United Counties RELLs with which I was familiar at home, those originating with Luton Corporation giving the most exhilarating ride (or not, if you were a pensioner laden down with shopping bags). Personal favourites, however, were the Plaxton-bodied RELH6Ls that were refurbished by Luton & District and put to work in their last year or so between Luton and Leighton Buzzard. I also had

a soft spot for the various RELLs that ran on Teesside from deregulation, operated by Delta, Thornaby, encountered when visiting the in-laws. These flogged up and down the Durham Road in Stockton, sporting various liveries. They were more fun to ride on than the usual Fleetline provided by competing Cleveland Transit (and cheaper too!).

This book is not intended as an in-depth history of the Bristol RE, as this has been done before (see Bibliography); rather, it is a celebration of Britain's most successful rear-engined single-deck bus, in its various guises, on the streets over the past 40 years, albeit concentrating on the 1970s, when the type was most ubiquitous. I could probably have filled a book with pictures taken around deregulation, but the condition of many would scarcely have been worthy of the 'Heyday' title!

Thanks are due to the photographers who have once again come to my aid. As always, when embarking on a book project, one can be quite blasé and assume that pictures would be easy to come by. A little way into the project and reality sets in, and you discover how poor your own collection is! A thankyou also to Paul Cripps of Ian Allan for his expert editing of my ramblings. Finally, the usual thanks to my wife; come to think of it, we did a fair bit of our courting on the local Bristol REs …

Kevin Lane
Dunstable
June 2008

Bibliography

The following publications have been useful in the compilation of this volume:

The Bristol RE — A Family Profile
  by Simon Butler (Trevallan Books, 1987)
Bristol RE — 40 years of service
  by Duncan Roberts (NBC Books, 2002)
Chassis List: Bristol RE Models
  (PSV Circle, 2000)
The British Bus Story: Early 'Seventies
  by Alan Townsin (TPC, 1987)
Lincolnshire Road Car 75
  by Graham Wise (NBC Books, 2003)
National Bus Company — the Early Years
  by Kevin Lane (Ian Allan Publishing, 2004)

Various 'Fleet Histories' published by the PSV Circle
Various editions of *Buses* and *Buses Extra* magazines (Ian Allan Publishing)
Various editions of *Classic Bus* magazine (Classic Bus Publishing)
Various NBC timetables

The following website was also useful:

http://bcv.robsly.com
  This is the website of Bristol Commercial Vehicle Enthusiasts and details, amongst other things, surviving Bristol buses.

The Bristol RE — a brief history

By the beginning of the 1960s single-deck buses and coaches had their engines either at the front (with forward control) or amidships. Although the rear-engined double-decker had been in production for several years, it took new legislation in 1961 to permit an increase in the length of single-deck buses to 36ft. This extra length could accommodate more passengers and, with the engine positioned behind the rear axle, a lower floor and wider entrance also. Although both AEC and Leyland introduced rear-engined models in 1964, it was the nationalised Bristol Commercial Vehicles which, perhaps against the odds, came out with the Bristol RE, in 1962.

There were three prototype RE chassis, numbered REX001-003.

REX001 was an RELL, signifying a long chassis with a low floor for bus work, and, as United BR1 (7431 HN), materialised in September 1962, fitted with a 54-seat ECW body. (The Bristol K double-decker, many of which would be replaced by the RE, seated 55.) This bodywork was to a new design but was unmistakably a product of Lowestoft. Power was provided by a Gardner 6HLX engine, mounted horizontally behind the rear (Lodekka) axle, below the frame. The five-speed synchromesh gearbox, newly designed and built in-house, was mounted ahead of the rear axle, allowing the engine to be set close to the other side and thus reducing rear overhang. Air suspension was provided for both axles.

REX002 was an RELH, again a long chassis but with a higher floor, more suited to coaching and express work (with motorways now a reality). Another new design of bodywork, seating 47, was provided by ECW, although this resembled a lengthened version of that fitted to the Bristol MW. The Gardner 6HLX engine was again utilized, and the vehicle joined the South Midland fleet in April 1963, registered 521 ABL.

REX003 was used by Bristol as a testbed. It was powered by a Bristol engine, making it an RELH6B, although a Gardner engine was substituted when it was completed in March 1967 as an ECW-bodied coach for West Yorkshire Road Car, with which it entered service as CRG1 (OWT 241E).

The prototypes having proved themselves, production commenced in 1963 with RELH chassis. Bristol Omnibus, appropriately, received the first of

these in October, for its Greyhound coach fleet. Vehicles delivered during the first year were all coaches (or dual-purpose vehicles, in the case of three for Midland General), allocated to various THC (Tilling) fleets, among them Eastern National, United, Western/Southern National and Crosville. The first production RELL buses appeared from September 1964, early recipients including United, Thames Valley, West Yorkshire and Lincolnshire. It should be mentioned at this stage that, as Bristol was a nationalised company, its customers were restricted to other nationalised companies (its lorries, for example, being available only for British Road Services).

Series I vehicles were delivered up until July 1967, some variety from the standard ECW body styles being provided by the Alexander bodies built on RELH6G chassis for Scottish Omnibuses and Western Scottish. With the exception of seven Leyland-engined RELH6Ls built for Bristol Omnibus in mid-1967, all Series I chassis, which ran to a total of 445, featured Gardner 6HLX or 6HLW power units.

In 1966 the purchase of a 25% stake in Bristol Commercial Vehicles by the Leyland Motor Corporation allowed any operator to buy products from either Bristol or ECW. With the potential for new customers, the RE was updated to incorporate a choice of specifications, such as semi-automatic transmission and leaf springs. A Leyland engine could also be requested, a popular choice for previous customers of Leyland buses who decided to buy the RE. At the same time new variants were announced, offering three further wheelbase options, including the shorter 16ft 2in RESL and RESH models.

By this time the RE faced competition from rival rear-engined single-deck chassis in the form of the Leyland Panther and AEC Swift. Nevertheless, Bristol gathered some impressive orders during 1966, including the municipal fleets at Coventry, Luton, Accrington and Newport, independent Lancashire United Transport and BET subsidiaries Southdown and North Western Road Car. The latter, at one time a Tilling company, had bought Bristol buses right up until the nationalisation of BCV in 1948 and was no doubt happy to be able to start buying them again!

The majority of the first wave of Series II chassis were RESL1 buses, the RESH2 amounting to just 11 in

total, delivered in 1967/8. The choice of bodywork would not necessarily fall to ECW either, some of these early orders going to Plaxton, Marshall and East Lancs. In turn, ECW would also build bodies for chassis other than Bristol. Bristol would now also be able to appear at the Commercial Motor Show, which it did in September 1966, after an absence of some 18 years.

Offered alongside the RESL1 was the RESL5, similar but with a 6in increase in the front overhang, allowing room for a wider entrance and thus qualifying for New Bus Grant. Of this variant 165 were built between mid-1967 and the beginning of 1970, the majority going to United, Crosville and Lancashire United.

In 1967 came the first Series II RELL buses, designated RELL3, production of which was to continue until 1983, reaching a total of 2,656. The later production, from 1976, was destined either for New Zealand or Northern Ireland.

Production of Series II RELH chassis, designated RELH4, also commenced in 1967, and customers included independent operators, Flight, Birmingham and Byng, Portsmouth, taking one each. However, although three RELHs were sold in Ireland, and the very last, in June 1975, to Davies of Halewood, smaller operators were not generally attracted to the RE, preferring lightweight chassis from Bedford, Ford, etc. The majority therefore went to the THC fleets and subsequently to the National Bus Company. In the case of the latter, they were destined mainly for former THC fleets, the Leyland Leopard remaining more popular with erstwhile BET subsidiaries. Bodywork was supplied, in the main, by ECW or Plaxton, along with a handful from Duple. In 1972 there appeared a new style of ECW coach body which, although distinctive, owed more than a nod to Plaxton's contemporary Panorama Elite design. It remained in production on the RELH until 1974, by which time 85 chassis had been so bodied. One of these, Tillings VHK 177L, would later have its body rebuilt by ECW as the prototype for the B51 design built in the early 1980s on Leyland Leopard and Tiger chassis.

The RELL6 chassis variant, with 17ft 6in wheelbase, amounted to just 44 vehicles delivered in 1967/8 to Reading (42) and Warrington (2). Those for Reading, fitted with box-like 'standee' bodywork (seating just 34) by Strachans or Pennine, had the dubious distinction of being the only REs to be used as trolleybus replacements.

A new and impressive RE variant was to hit the road early in 1969. The maximum length of a PSV was increased in 1967 from 11 to 12 metres, resulting in the REMH, a vehicle perhaps more suitable for the motorway age. The majority of the 104 chassis built were destined for Scottish Omnibuses and Western Scottish for their overnight Anglo-Scottish services, for which Alexander produced a new style of bodywork, very striking for its day, with raked-forward window pillars; designated the M type, the design would be perpetuated on the Seddons and Volvos that supplemented the REMHs on these services. The only other REMH chassis, fitted with rather less flamboyant bodywork by Plaxton, went to United in 1971/3/4 in three batches.

The final chassis variant was the RESL8, produced between 1970 and 1976. This was broadly similar to the RESL1 but was 4in longer in the wheelbase. Vehicles were supplied to NBC, PTE and municipal customers and to independent Lancashire United, although the last for NBC were delivered at the end of 1972, to United.

By this time the Leyland National, built by a new company owned jointly by Leyland and NBC, was entering service, and further orders for bus versions of the RE, from NBC in particular, were being actively discouraged. The very last Bristol REs to be delivered to an NBC subsidiary were Plaxton-bodied RELH6Gs for National Travel South East in May 1975.

Bristol RE production was to continue but only for export markets, the model being denied to loyal followers in the UK. A number of municipal operators bought the RE right up until the end, but no dispensation could be made for them; after all, they could always buy Leylands instead. Only two customers continued to buy the RE, no doubt to the annoyance of Leyland, these being the Christchurch Transport Board in New Zealand and Citybus/Ulsterbus in Northern Ireland, the latter, in response to a threat to turn to Mercedes-Benz, having

Right: Bristol REs were most commonly found in NBC fleets but made popular second-hand buys for independents — sometimes after surprisingly short careers with their original owners. Silver Service RESL6L/ECW 63 (JEH 193K), seen on 21 June 1981 outside its operator's garage in Darley Dale, Derbyshire, had been new nine years earlier as Potteries Motor Traction 193. *Charles Dean / Author's collection*

been reclassified by Leyland an export market! The last examples — RELL6Gs — were finally delivered to Citybus in June 1984.

As far as the National Bus Company was concerned, the first Bristol RE withdrawals began in the late 1970s as the early examples became life-expired. These gathered pace in the 1980s, hastened by the implementation of Market Analysis Project (MAP) and, later, the widespread introduction minibuses. This period also saw REs transferred between subsidiaries as traffic requirements changed, one interesting example concerning Lincolnshire Road Car; such was the state of the company's finances that it disposed of late-model RELH coaches with expired certificates of fitness in 1984 and acquired from Northern RELH6Ls that were still roadworthy! Some NBC companies, notably Badgerline, the new North Western, Potteries and Luton & District, retained REs following privatisation, although by the end of the 1980s most had gone, many seeing further service with independents that sprang up following de-regulation in 1986 (often running alongside early Leyland Nationals, also deposed from NBC service. Notable among these operators were Northern Bus, Sheffield, and Delta, Stockton. A few operators organised a final farewell; Southern National,

for example, had a 'Last RE Running Day' on 7 March 1987, using two choice examples, RELL6G 2702 and RELH6G 1468, with a combined age of 37!

Municipal REs were also in decline during the 1980s (although the last user, Hartlepool Transport, retained its final examples until 1997); however, it was during this decade also that some municipal operators acquired their first REs, Ipswich and Southend, for instance, taking RELLs from Leicester and Hants & Dorset respectively, whilst others, like Blackburn, increased their stock, in this case from Ribble. Particularly interesting was Busways (successor to Tyne & Wear PTE), which bought REs in some quantity from such sources as Colchester, Merseyside and Thamesdown, viewing them as a better investment (and aided by a mountain of spares from United and Northern!) than Leyland Nationals or Leopards.

More than 45 years after the first Bristol RE hit the road, the type is now all but extinct in normal service, but around 200 survive in preservation in one state or another, and an increasing number are appearing at bus rallies. Several RELLs survive in Belfast, operating for City Sightseeing, but to see REs at work in any quantity requires a trip to New Zealand, where ex-Christchurch RELLs can still be encountered.

Above: Of operators in mainland Britain Bristol Omnibus Co and its subsidiaries took the greatest number of Bristol REs — 425 in total, mostly RELLs. The first four RELL/ECW buses were allocated to Cheltenham District, including 1001 (KHW 307E), pictured at Bishops Cleeve beside another red classic in the shape of a K6 telephone box before returning to the town centre in June 1969. *Colin Martin*

Above right: Less than a year old, having been delivered the previous April, RELL6L/ECW 1280 (EHU 381K) negotiates Swindon in the midst of redevelopment on 9 February 1973, having arrived from Wroughton. The attractive livery style, with a greater area of cream than hitherto, had been introduced in 1969 to distinguish one-man-operated buses. *John Jones*

Right: Swindon was also home to the only municipal Bristol REs in the West of England, five having been bought by Thamesdown in 1975. This was very late in the day for the model, and these vehicles, all RESL6Gs, were amongst only a handful to receive 'P'-suffix registrations as well as being the last REs to be bodied by ECW. No 166 (JMW 166P) stands in a damp Fleming Way on 17 February 1977. It would later run for Busways, in that operator's Blue Bus Services fleet. *John Jones*

Left: Seventy-three Bristol RELLs were delivered to Southern/Western National in the period 1967-73. The first eight — all for Southern National — included 2701 (HDV 627E), seen in Yeovil on 16 March 1973, by which time the Southern National Omnibus Co had been absorbed by its larger neighbour. Sister vehicle 2700, for many years a Yeovil bus, has been preserved since 1986. *John Jones*

Above: The Western National fleet received its first Bristol RELH/ECW coaches in 1964 and continued to take this combination, mainly for Royal Blue work, until 1970, whereafter bodywork was supplied by Plaxton. New in 1968 in traditional Royal Blue colours, ECW-bodied 1450 (LDV 468F) is seen while on tour in Falmouth in the summer of 1971, having been repainted in the style of livery initially devised by NBC for express coaches serving the South West. *John Aldridge*

Left: Formerly a BET company, Devon General had no Bristol tradition prior to the NBC era, but in 1974, by which time it was little more than a division of Western National, it was allocated four Bristol RELH6G/Plaxton coaches. Unusually for the type these were delivered in 'local coach' livery. No 2501 (PUO 501M) manœuvres out of Exeter bus station on 23 April 1976. *John Jones*

Left: Following the division in 1983 of the Western National Omnibus Co its surviving Bristol REs found themselves with new owners. North Devon Ltd, based in Barnstaple and trading as Red Bus, inherited 21, to which it added further examples from West Yorkshire Road Car. Still in poppy red (as opposed to the darker shade adopted by its new owner), RELL6G/ECW 2775 (VWT 680L) waits in the rain outside the travel office on The Quay, Bideford, *c*1984. *Chris Lodington collection*

Right: Of the NBC coaching subsidiaries combined early in 1974 to form National Travel (South West) two had been customers for the Bristol RE. Exeter-based Greenslades Tours took 10 RELH6Ls (five in Grey Cars livery) in 1971 and five more in 1973, all bodied by Plaxton. No 303 (UFJ 232J), of the first batch, is seen on a tour to Scotland when still quite new. *Author's collection*

Right: Black & White Motorways' contribution to the National Travel (South West) fleet included seven Plaxton-bodied RELH6Gs, these being a cancelled Western National order received in 1972. Fresh from Associated Motorways duty, 334 (ADG 334K) rests in the yard behind Cheltenham Coach Station on 25 February 1973. *John Jones*

Left: Hants & Dorset received 55 ECW-bodied Bristol RELL6Gs in the period 1968-72. Delivered (in Tilling green) in 1970 as No 3039, 1635 (TRU 217J) is pictured in Ringwood on its way to Bournemouth on 5 August 1974. *Mike Greenwood*

Right: Perhaps more swansong than heyday: when Hants & Dorset was split, in April 1983, the new Wilts & Dorset Bus Co took over operations in its western area, along with a number of Bristol RELL6Gs, and of these 1626 (RLJ 345H) was still hard at work five years later, being seen in Poole on 16 April 1988. Sister vehicle 1622 survives in preservation. *Graham Wise / Author's collection*

Right: Hitherto independent Provincial joined the NBC fold in 1970 and soon received Bristol REs. The first six, which arrived in 1971, were diverted from Hants & Dorset in exchange for Daimler Fleetlines, while a further six, delivered the following year, had been intended for Northern General. Among the latter was 11 (ECG 111K), pictured at its operator's Hoeford depot on 28 June 1975. Sister vehicle 12 survives in preservation, restored to its original livery of emerald green and cream. *John Jones*

Left: Southern Vectis took a modest number of Bristol REs for bus work, these amounting to eight RESL6G and nine RELL6G variants, all with ECW bodywork. Representing the former is flat-screen 815 (NDL 767G), pictured at Carisbrook Castle in June 1971. *John Aldridge*

Left: Southern Vectis' later RE buses were of the longer RELL variety. No 866 (TDL 566K), of the final batch of seven, is pictured *c*1974 in Newport bus station. *Author's collection*

Right: Generally favouring Bedford chassis as the basis for its coaches, Southern Vectis took just two REs for such work, the first being 301 (KDL 885F), a rare RESH6G/Duple, new in 1968. The other was 302 (XDL 122L), an ECW-bodied RELH6G delivered in 1972 and seen here on layover in Ryde on 1 June 1977. Upon withdrawal, in 1988, 302 passed into preservation only to be snapped up by Northern Bus, of North Anston, near Sheffield, where it was twice re-registered, but in 1996 it returned to preservation, regaining its original identity. No 301 is also preserved but by contrast has remained on the Isle of Wight. *Charles Dean / Author's collection*

15

In the summer of 1968 Brighton, Hove & District took into stock 10 dual-door Bristol RESL6G/ECW buses, which joined an otherwise all-double-deck fleet. All passed to Southdown with effect from 1 January 1969. With Leyland PD3s of Southdown and Brighton Corporation looking on, 2210 (PPM 210G) — new as BH&D 210 — is pictured in Brighton's Old Steine in June 1973. Both this vehicle and similar 2206 have been preserved. *John Aldridge*

Right: A loyal Leyland supporter, Southdown was nevertheless quick to specify Bristol chassis when these became available, placing an initial order for 40 Marshall-bodied RESLs for delivery in 1968. The company eventually amassed a total of 86 REs (including vehicles inherited from BH&D); one of a final trio delivered in 1971, RELL6L/ECW 492 (UCD 602J) had been ordered as part of a batch of 10, the other seven being diverted to Thames/Alder Valley. It was photographed in Brighton on 17 August 1983, ready to depart for Eastbourne on the inland route via Lewes. *John Young*

Right: The easternmost extremities of Sussex saw no Bristol RE operations by a major operator until 1986, when Hastings & District, split from Maidstone & District in May 1983, acquired its first examples, a pair of ECW-bodied RESLs from Ribble. To these it added further REs from various sources, among them 412 (AHT 212J), an RELL6L/ECW new to Bristol Omnibus but acquired from Badgerline in 1988. It is seen at Rye station in September 1989. *David Taylor / John Jones collection*

Left: Having been amongst the first customers for the RE, taking early examples of both the RELL and the RELH, Thames Valley in March 1968 received eight RESL5 variants with dual-door ECW bodywork. Still looking smart, S331 (LJB 331F) was photographed that September in Maidenhead. *Mike Sutcliffe*

Left: Another erstwhile BET subsidiary to turn to Bristol for its rear-engined single-deckers was Aldershot & District, which prior to the merger with Thames Valley in 1972 took both RELLs and RESLs. New in 1971 as Aldershot & District 627 and still in its original owner's attractive livery of two-tone green and cream (contrasting with a similar bus alongside in poppy red), Alder Valley RELL6G/Marshall 443 (YHO 627J) is pictured at Aldershot on 14 March 1973. *John Jones*

Below: Reading Corporation took to the Bristol RELL6G with some enthusiasm, receiving 42 as trolleybus replacements in 1967/8. These buses represented all but two of the rare 17ft 6in-wheelbase RELL6 variant (Warrington taking the other pair) and were bodied by Strachans and Pennine. This unusual view at Mill Lane depot in September 1982 features 263/5 (KRD 263/5F), both with Strachans bodywork, alongside another Bristol product, VRTLL6G/Northern Counties 20 (XRD 20J). *Author*

Left: Chassis REX002, effectively the prototype RELH6G, went to South Midland Motor Services as its 867 (521 ABL), being seen here resplendent at Oxford's Gloucester Green bus station before departing for London in April 1968. Alongside is Thames Valley RELH6G/ECW C405 (835 CRX), one of a pair delivered in February 1964. *Mike Sutcliffe*

Above: Previously a coaching subsidiary of Thames Valley, Oxford-based South Midland passed to the control of City of Oxford with effect from 1 January 1971 and thereafter became little more than a supplementary fleetname. However, upon the division of COMS in 1984 the South Midland name was restored to greater prominence, being used for a new company operating from Abingdon, Bicester, Wantage and Witney. Bristol RELH6L/ECW coach 89 (RBW 89M), new in 1974 to City of Oxford, arrives in Coventry *c*1985. *Author's collection*

Left: The first Bristol REs for Eastern National were 15 RELH6G/ECW coaches delivered early in 1964. Originally numbered 583, 405 (AVX 966B) heads through Coventry in August 1975. *Tom Moore*

Above: Some 55 Bristol RELL6G/ECW buses were bought by Eastern National between 1969 and 1972. New in October 1969, 1510 (FVX 612H) was photographed in Colchester in July 1978; having arrived from Clacton, a 20-mile journey taking 50 minutes, it is about to embark on the 2½-hour, 40-mile marathon to Southend via Maldon — an experience likely to be appreciated by only the most diehard of RE enthusiasts! *Geoff Mills*

Left: An unusual customer for the Bristol RELH6L was Isle of Man Road Services, which took a pair with Duple bodies in May 1970, followed a year later by two with Plaxton. They saw relatively little use on the island, and early in 1973 all four were acquired by London-based NBC coaching subsidiary Samuelson's, passing thence to National Travel (South East) in 1974. Seen at Eastern National's Central Works at Chelmsford on 17 March 1973 is Duple-bodied 38 UMN, which prior to entering service on the mainland would be re-registered as SGF 485L. *Geoff Mills*

Left: New to Eastern National (430) but placed in the Tilling fleet with effect from 1 January 1971, Bristol RELH6G/Plaxton 9430 (LWC 981J) worked thereafter from Prittlewell, where it was based when this photograph was taken. On 1 April 1973 operations would be transferred to Kelvedon, subsequently being merged with those of Samuelson's and Timpson's to form National Travel (South East). *Author's collection*

Right: The first and last Series II RELH chassis (101 and 766) both gravitated to Essex. Plaxton-bodied JON 700E, the RELH6L that had been delivered to Flight, Birmingham as an executive coach in 1967, is seen here in Southend in 1979, operating with Alpine, Chadwell Heath. Sadly this vehicle would later be destroyed in an arson attack. *Geoff Mills*

Right: JNK 561N, also Plaxton-bodied but as an RELH6G, passed to S&M Coaches, of Benfleet. Pictured in February 1985, it had been new 10 years earlier to Davies of Halewood, Merseyside. The updated Supreme IV lower front panels and side mouldings blend surprisingly well with the Panorama Elite body style. *Geoff Mills*

Above: Several municipal operators in East Anglia operated the Bristol RE, although only one, Colchester, bought the type new. Five RELL6Ls with ECW bodies joined the fleet in May 1972, to be followed by a further 10 during 1973. No 25 (SWC 25K), of the first batch, is seen at work in its home town on 1 April 1976. *Charles Dean / Author's collection*

Right: Both Ipswich and Southend acquired REs second-hand. Those at Ipswich — five RELL6Ls with dual-door ECW bodywork — came from another municipal source, Leicester, in 1980. No 122 (TRY 122H), photographed in its new home town on 31 August 1984, has since been preserved, as has similar 118. *John Young*

Above: Eastern Counties, which company's operating area included the Eastern Coach Works plant at Lowestoft, took 149 Bristol REs from new. The first bus versions were 14 ECW-bodied RESL6Gs delivered in 1967, among them RS648 (KVF 648E), seen at Norwich on 22 April 1972 and by now fitted with a Gardner 6HLW engine in place of its original 6HLX. Most of the batch would survive until 1981. *Maurice Doggett*

Above right: New in 1970, RLE869 (WPW 869H), a 1970 RELL6G with flat-screen, dual-purpose ECW body, was still in fine fettle some 14 years later, being pictured at Bawdsey Links, near Woodbridge, Suffolk, on 31 August 1984. This vehicle survives in preservation. *John Young*

Right: Eastern Counties took 11 Plaxton-bodied RELH6G coaches in the years 1971/3/4. With a full load, RLE856 (LPW 856L) grinds up Buckingham Palace Road, towards Victoria on a working from Norwich via Thetford and Newmarket in July 1982. *Charles Dean / Author's collection*

Left: United Counties took the Bristol RE between 1964 and 1974, both the first and last being RELH coaches. With the exception of the last five, which were Plaxton-bodied RELH6Ls, all other coaches were ECW-bodied RELH6Gs. No 276 (ORP 276F), new in 1968, calls at Market Harborough on 31 May 1975 while *en route* from Nottingham and London via Leicester and Northampton. *Chris Lodington*

Left: United Counties' RE buses, all ECW-bodied, were mainly RELLs with flat windscreens, the exceptions being seven RESLs delivered in 1971. New in 1968, RELL6G 323 (RBD 323G) heads into Luton from Dunstable in December 1985, mere days before division of the company. *Author*

Right: Upon the break-up of United Counties at the beginning of 1986 Luton & District found itself with 27 assorted Bristol REs, among them RELL6G/ECW 344 (URP 344H), seen here in Green Cross Code livery pulling away from the stop at Ashcroft, Dunstable, on its way to Luton Airport in May 1987. Behind is RELH6G/ECW 214 (KRP 214L), still in NBC dual-purpose livery but with '**LUTON BUS**' fleetnames. *Author*

Below: The oldest vehicle in the Luton & District fleet to wear the red-and-ivory livery was Bristol RELL6G/ECW 311 (NBD 311F), new in 1968. Seen heading through Dunstable in July 1986, it would be retained as a company-owned preserved vehicle following withdrawal from normal service in 1988. *Author*

Left: Luton Corporation was an early municipal customer for the RE, taking delivery of 30 Bristol RELL6Ls with dual-door ECW bodywork in 1967/8. However, their introduction was dogged with problems: one-man-operation was resisted by crews and unpopular with some passengers as it coincided with an increase in fares, while sabotage, in the form of sawdust in the fuel tanks, was also recorded. No 105 (MXD 105E) is pictured at Limbury on the first day of service, 2 July 1967. Ten further RELLs were on order when Luton was taken over by United Counties and these were delivered in 1970, being distinguishable from the initial 30 by their Northamptonshire (VNV) registrations, Gardner engines and deeper windscreens. *Chris Lodington*

Left: Leicester Corporation created a little oasis of Bristol operation in Midland Red territory with the introduction in 1967 of five dual-door ECW-bodied RESL6Ls, among them No 1 (LJF 1F), here being pursued through its home city by a similarly bodied Leyland Atlantean. There followed 23 RELL6Ls in the years 1968-70 (see page 27), after which Leicester turned for its single-deck requirements to the Metro-Scania. *Charles Dean / Author's collection*

Right: In 1965/6 Coventry Corporation hired several single-deckers to assess their suitability for one-man operation. One of these was a West Yorkshire Bristol RELL6G/ECW (HWU 641C), which led to an order for six RESL6Gs, also with ECW bodywork. Pictured in Warwick Road in 1971, single-door 518 (KHP 518E) shows off a recently applied revised livery of cherry red and cream. *Tom Moore*

Left: Midland General was an early operator of the Bristol RE, in May 1964 taking a trio of RELH6G/ECW coaches including 30 (1384 R), seen *en route* for Skegness in 1968. Note the sliding windows fitted in lieu of the more usual fixed glazing. *Mike Sutcliffe*

Above: Also in the Midland General fleet were the only RESH2 variants bodied by ECW (rather than Duple). The second of the pair of RESH6Gs delivered in October 1967, 134 (SRB 67F) was photographed heading through Mansfield in June 1968. Under Trent control from 1972, Midland General would continue to take REs, latterly in NBC poppy red, until 1974. *Mike Sutcliffe*

Above: The majority of the Bristol REs bought new by Trent Motor Traction, formerly a BET subsidiary, were dual-purpose vehicles or coaches, such as 268 (PCH 268L), a 1972 RELH6L with the second style of ECW coach body, seen on layover in Derby on 28 April 1973. *Charles Dean / Author's collection*

Right: Trent's stock of REs was increased considerably by vehicles acquired from Midland General and North Western. Ordered by the latter but delivered new to Trent, RELL6L/ECW 344 (LRC 344K) loads in Matlock on 1 May 1982. *Charles Dean / Author's collection*

Left: A BET company, East Midland Motor Services was denied the Bristol RE until 1967, when the first examples entered the fleet. No O520 (PNN 520F), an ECW-bodied RELL6G dating from 1968, is seen in St James Street, Doncaster on 20 September 1969. Its red-and-cream livery would later be superseded by NBC leaf green.
Roger Holmes

Right: Yet another BET company in the Midlands, Potteries Motor Traction took the RE only during the period 1971-3 yet managed to add 56 of the type to its fleet. One of a number to survive privatisation in 1986 was 222 (PVT 222L), an RELL6L/ECW, resplendent in the company's new livery as it passes St Chad's Church, Wybunbury, while *en route* from Walgherton to Crewe in July 1989.
Tony Moyes

Left: Although it bought the Bristol RE from 1964 until 1975 Lincolnshire Road Car took just 51 new examples, this total being split almost equally between buses and coaches. One of four RELL6Gs delivered in 1965, 1205 (AVL 738C) is seen leaving Doncaster for Scunthorpe on 21 May 1981. Similar 1208 survives in preservation as the oldest remaining RE bus. *Charles Dean / Author's collection*

Left: A further 15 REs were subsequently acquired second-hand, among them a quartet of 12-year-old Plaxton-bodied RELH6Ls received from Trent in 1985. Painted in its owner's attractive new 'local coach' livery of two-tone green and white, No 1435 (URC 958M) pulls out of the bus station at St Marks, Lincoln, in August 1986. *John Jones*

Right: Another operator within Lincolnshire to run the Bristol RE was Lincoln City Transport, which was very much a late-comer to the type, buying a dozen Alexander-bodied RELLs in two batches in 1973. Although all had been withdrawn by 1986, several were reinstated following deregulation, and 70 (RVL 70L) was photographed at Lincoln Central station on 19 June 1989 heading south across the level crossing (and infamous bottleneck) and past the fine signalbox of 1874. No 73 (UVL 873M), which left the fleet in 1982, survives in preservation. *John Young*

Right: Long-established independent operator W. Gash, of Newark, bought a pair of ECW-bodied Bristol RELL6Gs as part of its post-deregulation expansion, but the company was over-ambitious and in April 1988 was bought by Yorkshire Traction, which ran it as a separate operation. New to Western National in 1970, Gash BR6 (TUO 253J) was photographed at Newark on 10 September 1988. In 1989 control of the Gash operation would pass to Lincolnshire Road Car, itself by then owned by Yorkshire Traction. *Authors collection*

Above: The West Riding Automobile Co, at one time the country's largest independent operator, received five Plaxton-bodied Bristol RELL6Gs in 1969. By then, however, the company was in NBC ownership, having sold out to the Transport Holding Co in October 1967, and subsequent deliveries had more conventional ECW bodywork. Bound for Manchester, 325 (CHL 637K) was photographed alongside West Yorkshire 1240 (RWX 784F) at Bradford on 3 June 1973, by which time West Riding's green livery was giving way to NBC poppy red. *Charles Dean / Author's collection*

Right: To a later generation of enthusiasts the best-known operator of the Bristol RE in Yorkshire was an independent, Northern Bus of North Anston, successor to the old-established firm of Wigmore, Dinnington. Around 70 examples of the type were owned at one time or another, either for operational use or for spares, seeing service in and around the Sheffield area following deregulation. There were many livery variations, including the short-lived 'Bradfield Bus' scheme applied to RELL6G/ECW 2182 (SJA 382K), seen working from Stocksbridge towards Sheffield near the village of Ewden Valley on 16 October 1993. New to North Western Road Car shortly before the division of that company, whereupon it passed to Crosville, this vehicle survives today in preservation. *Bob Telfer*

One of the largest users of the Bristol RE in Yorkshire was the West Yorkshire Road Car
Co, which took more than 200. The majority of these were of the RELL3 type,
including 1363 (MWW 756K), seen basking in the sun at Bradford on 3 June 1973.
Charles Dean / Author's collection

Above: In 1977/8 seven of West Yorkshire's RELH6G coaches had their ECW bodywork 'updated' by Willowbrook, although whether this was an improvement æsthetically is a matter of opinion. No 1025 (YYG 217G) is seen resplendent at Skipton on 21 May 1978. *Author's collection*

Right: In September 1986 United's Scarborough operations passed to East Yorkshire. Arguably the most unusual vehicle transferred was a Bristol RELL6G that had had its ECW body converted to open-top in 1985. Formerly United 4278, East Yorkshire 600 (PHN 178L) was photographed on 25 June 1993 in an approximation of its new owner's traditional livery of dark blue and primrose. *John Aldridge*

45

Above: The largest operator of the Bristol RE in mainland Britain was ex-Tilling Group company United Automobile Services, which between 1962 and 1975 took no fewer than 470 examples, and these could be found throughout Northumberland, County Durham and North Yorkshire as well as further afield on coaching work. Included in this total was the very first RE, (chassis REX001), an RELL6G fitted with an ECW 54-seat bus body; registered 7431 HN, it entered service at Darlington in December 1962 numbered BR1 but is seen here in Newcastle on 20 January 1975, by which time it had been renumbered as 4101. Based latterly at Blyth, this historic vehicle was set aside for preservation following withdrawal in 1979 but sadly has not survived. *Charles Dean / Author's collection*

Above right: Prior to the introduction of the National white, United's coaching fleet wore an attractive livery of olive green and cream, shown here on Bristol RELH6G/ECW 1238 (JHN 838D) on private-hire work at Newcastle's Marlborough Street bus station on 8 August 1972. *Charles Dean / Author's collection*

Right: United was the only English customer for the 12m REMH chassis, taking 35 Plaxton-bodied examples in the years 1971/3/4. One of the first batch was 1304 (GHN 204J), photographed in April 1973. *Author's collection*

Left: Northern General and its subsidiaries, being BET companies, were initially denied the Bristol RE. However, in NBC days 33 ECW-bodied RELL6Gs were ordered for delivery in 1971 — 23 for the main fleet, six for Gateshead & District and four for Tynemouth. Wearing its operator's attractive pre-NBC livery style, Northern 2740 (KCN 240J) is seen on layover in Newcastle. Northern would soon be seduced by the charms of the Leyland National, ending any hope of further deliveries of Bristol saloons. *Charles Dean / Author's collection*

Left: Tynemouth's allocation of four RELLs was transferred almost immediately to the main fleet; indeed, the last of the quartet, intended as Tynemouth 319, was delivered direct to Northern; 2790 (KFT 919J) was nevertheless still in Tynemouth colours when photographed on 17 January 1975. In common with all of Northern's RE buses it was to have a short career, being withdrawn in 1981 despite rebuilding to single-door in 1979. *Charles Dean / Author's collection*

Right: Later Bristol RE deliveries to the Northern group were restricted to RELH6L coaches, 14 arriving in 1972 with ECW's new-style coach bodywork in Northern's pre-NBC coach livery. In common with many coaches during the NBC era they then ran for several years in white before succumbing to dual-purpose liveries; however, these vehicles went one further, at the end of their lives receiving bus livery of all-over red or yellow, as demonstrated by 4886 (MCN 886L) at Stanley bus station on 9 February 1982. All were withdrawn and sold by early 1983. *Charles Dean / Author's collection*

Right: The Northern group's final REs were 10 RELH6G/Plaxton coaches delivered in 1973, of which two were allocated initially to the Sunderland District fleet. Although painted in National white, they were fitted for one-man-operation; No 122L (NCN 822L) catches the late-afternoon sun as it leaves its home town on 19 November 1974. Both vehicles would pass to Northern upon the latter's absorption of Sunderland District at the beginning of 1975. *Charles Dean / Author's collection*

Left: Three municipal operators in the North East took the Bristol RE. On Tyneside, two batches of ECW-bodied RESLs were placed into service by South Shields Corporation in 1967/8, entering a wholly double-deck fleet. The first batch (1-5) had curved fronts, the second (6-12) flat. At the beginning of 1970 the South Shields fleet was combined with that of neighbouring Newcastle under the stewardship of the newly formed Tyneside PTE, which soon developed a preference for double-deckers, and no further orders for REs were forthcoming. Originally South Shields 10, Tyneside 980 (HCU 520G) is seen in typical wintry conditions in Newcastle on 27 March 1975. All 12 buses were withdrawn in 1977, although one, ECU 201E, would return to serve in the post-deregulation Busways fleet and is now preserved. *Charles Dean / Author's collection*

Left: From the mid-1960s Sunderland Corporation pursued a policy of buying high-capacity 'standee' single-deckers, including 10 RELL6Gs with 47-seat bodywork by Metro-Cammell (a combination destined to remain unique), which arrived in 1968. In 1973 the Sunderland fleet was absorbed by Tyneside PTE (which thus became Tyne & Wear PTE), allowing its vehicles to broaden their sphere of operations; new as Sunderland 103, Tyne & Wear 903 (JBR 103F) was thus engaged on contract work at Gateshead's Tyne Valley Trading Estate when photographed on 2 November 1975. This vehicle would be among eight REs acquired for further use with Burnley & Pendle (see page 58). *Charles Dean / Author's collection*

Towards the end of the 1980s the Bristol RE enjoyed something of a revival on
Tyneside, Busways (successor to Tyne & Wear PTE) acquiring a number of the type
to operate low-cost services in the wake of deregulation. The majority were late-
model RESL6Ls from Merseyside and Thamesdown and RELL6Ls from Colchester;
from the last-named came 1811 (YWC 18L), pictured in Sunderland while working
from South Shields in June 1989. *Geoff Mills*

Above: Hartlepool Corporation, formed in April 1967 by the merging of the Borough of Hartlepool and the County Borough of West Hartlepool, was a prolific user of the Bristol RE. The first batch of seven ECW-bodied RELL6Ls arrived during the summer of 1967, and by 1975 further vehicles, replacing a largely double-deck fleet, had brought the total to 58; no doubt more would have been bought had the type remained available. Flat-screen 50 (HEF 50F) shows the original livery style on 14 October 1975. *Charles Dean / Author's collection*

Right: Hartlepool's REs were to have long lives, outlasting a number of more modern vehicles; indeed, the later examples would doubtless have survived even longer had not Hartlepool sold out to Stagecoach in 1994. Pictured in September 1997, No 93 (JAJ 293N), from the final, 1975 batch, was destined to be the last RE in service, being withdrawn two months after the photograph was taken. *Author*

Left: Cumberland Motor Services, a little Tilling outpost in the extreme North West of England received its first REs — a pair of RELL6Gs — in 1966. One of this initial pair, 251 (JAO 251D), was photographed on 23 September 1978, a year before withdrawal. *Charles Dean / Author's collection*

Left: All subsequent REs for Cumberland were Leyland-engined, all bar one being RELL6Ls. The exception, delivered in 1972, was dual-purpose RELH6L/ECW 600 (DRM 600K), seen at Whitehaven garage in June 1984. Destined to be withdrawn the following year, it was by now in its fourth and final Cumberland livery — and arguably the least attractive. *Charles Dean / Author's collection*

In 1968 came the first Bristol REs for Ribble, hitherto a BET company and which
previously had bought little else but Leylands, and between then and 1972 some 139
examples were placed in service. The majority were RESL6Ls, delivered in 1971/2
with bodywork by either Marshall or ECW; representing both styles at Burnley
on 15 June 1985 are Marshall-bodied 317 (LRN 317J) and ECW-bodied 337
(NCK 337J). *Graeme Yuill*

A number of Lancashire municipalities took the Bristol RE in preference to the unreliable Panther offered by their traditional supplier, Leyland. Fylde Borough Council (formerly Lytham St Annes Corporation) was very late to the party, buying just five ECW-bodied RESL6Ls in 1975. No 40 (HRN 107N) basks in the spring sunshine of 18 April 1982. *Charles Dean / Author's collection*

Right: Darwen bought seven RESL6Ls, all with East Lancs bodywork, in the period 1971-3. No 3 (STC 889L) was photographed on 21 April 1973, a year before the merger of Darwen's tiny fleet with that of neighbouring Blackburn. *John Jones*

Right: Having bought no new REs, Blackburn acquired seven RESLs upon the merger with Darwen in 1974, to which it added five from Leicester in 1978 (replacing Seddon RUs) and six (received in exchange for Leyland Atlantean double-deckers) from Ribble in 1986. Formerly Ribble 367, 405 (OCK 367K) is pictured near Whalley, between Blackburn and Clitheroe, in June 1988. *Tony Moyes*

Left: Between 1970 and 1974 Burnley, Colne & Nelson and its successor, Burnley & Pendle, took a total of 25 Bristol RESLs. BC&N 107 (PHG 807K), an RESL6L with Pennine bodywork, was photographed on 31 March 1973. *Charles Dean / Author's collection*

Left: In 1977 and 1979 Burnley & Pendle acquired from Tyne & Wear PTE eight Metro-Cammell-bodied RELL6Gs that had originated with Sunderland Corporation. Looking smart in the brighter Burnley & Pendle livery, 94 (JBR 100F) was photographed on 19 July 1981. *Charles Dean / Author's collection*

Right: In the period 1968-75 Accrington Corporation and its successor, Hyndburn Transport, received 13 East Lancs-bodied RESLs. This was the first, 25 (MTJ 925G), seen in its home town on 21 April 1973. *John Jones*

Right: Another Lancashire convert to the Bristol RE was Rossendale, which in the mid-1970s took nine East Lancs-bodied RESL6Ls. One of the second batch, of four, delivered in 1975, 11 (JDK 911P) was photographed in Rawtenstall on 14 June 1985. *Graham Yuill*

Above: Although SELNEC PTE did not buy any new REs it inherited vehicles from the Stalybridge, Hyde, Mossley & Dukinfield Joint Board and the North Western Road Car Co. SHMD provided just six— Northern Counties-bodied RESL6Gs dating from 1967. SELNEC 5078 (YLG 718F), formerly SHMD 118, stands outside the garage at Stalybridge on 22 April 1973. Sister vehicle 117 survives in preservation. *John Jones*

Right: An noteworthy customer for the RE was independent Lancashire United Transport, which took 50 RESL6Gs in three batches (in 1967, 1969 and 1974) with bodywork by Plaxton (the only examples on RESL chassis) or Alexander. Plaxton-bodied 259 (CTE 485E), one of the first batch, is seen in Wigan in August 1977, by which time LUT had become a subsidiary of Greater Manchester (formerly SELNEC) PTE. *Roger Holmes*

Left: In 1969 Liverpool Corporation, already a major user of the Leyland Panther, took delivery of 25 Park Royal-bodied RELL6Gs, and to these were added 20 ECW-bodied RESL6Ls under the auspices of Merseyside PTE in 1971 and 1975. Of the latter batch, 2147 (GTJ 383N) is seen at work in St Helens in September 1985.
Tony Moyes

Left: Widnes Corporation, despite its history as an operator of Leylands, bought eight Bristol RESL6L and three RELL6L buses with East Lancs bodies in the years 1971-3, to be followed by four further RELL6Ls, delivered to its successor, Halton Transport, in 1975. No 52 (CTD 52J) one of the initial pair, is seen at work in the town on 24 March 1973.
John Jones

Warrington — another municipality that might otherwise have remained a loyal
Leyland customer (having received four Panther Cubs in 1967) — bought 25 Bristol
REs between 1968 and 1976. One of seven East Lancs-bodied RESL6Ls delivered
in 1972, No 2 (YED 275K) was pictured in Northwich on 2 June 1973.
Following deregulation Warrington would buy RELLs second-hand from Lincoln.
Charles Dean / Author's collection

Above: At one time a Tilling company but from 1942 part of the BET Federation, North Western escaped nationalisation in 1948 but was thus denied Bristol chassis until 1966. Thereafter it took to the RE with enthusiasm, adding some 109 REs to stock between 1967 and 1972. One of the first batch, comprising 40 Marshall-bodied RESL6Gs, 285 (KJA 285F) is seen in company with two similar vehicles at Stockport on 11 August 1972, still in NWRCC red but with SELNEC Cheshire fleetnames, following the dismembering of North Western earlier in the year. *Charles Dean / Author's collection*

Left: Later REs for North Western were RELLs with bodywork by Alexander, Marshall or ECW. Nine ECW-bodied RELL6Ls delivered in 1971 featured a low-profile roof that permitted them to pass under the 8ft 9in Bridgewater Canal bridge at Dunham Woodhouses, one such being 377 (SJA 377J), seen on layover at Buxton when almost new. Following collapse in 1973 the bridge would be rebuilt to accommodate normal single-deckers. *Bill Potter*

Left: Chepstow-based Red & White Services received its first Bristol REs in 1965 and continued to take the type until 1974. Prominent in this photograph, taken in Cardiff bus station early in 1973, is RELL6L/ECW R567 (LAX 126F), whilst behind are a pair of RESL6Ls, that nearer the camera being RS967 (LAX 109E). All date from 1967, but R567 carries the later style of ECW body, with flat windscreen, which appeared first on the longer chassis. *Colin Martin*

Left: The Red & White fleet also included a number Bristol RELH6Ls. Many of the later examples were dual-purpose vehicles with coach seating inside bus-shell ECW bodywork, among them RD4672 (CWO 295K), seen loading in Newport on 3 April 1976. *Charles Dean / Author's collection*

Hitherto independent Jones of Aberbeeg was taken over by NBC in April 1969 and placed under Red & White control. It was, however, allowed to retain its blue livery. Eight Bristol REs were allocated to the company, six being RELH6L coaches, the other two RELL6L buses. One of the latter, R3671 (YWO 691K), loads at Newport for Ebbw Vale on 3 April 1976. *Charles Dean / Author's collection*

Left: On 20 April 1978 Red & White and Western Welsh were merged to form a new company, National Welsh. The last REs for Red & White were six ECW-bodied RELH6Ls, new in 1974. RD1138 (OWO 305M), showing the Welsh version of the fleetname, pulls away from Cheltenham Coach Station in this early-1980s view, working the 15.00 to Aberdare, where it was timed to arrive at 18.20. In the background is Crosville (ex-Ribble) RELH6L/ECW ERL529 (PTF 711L), which had arrived as the 10.50 from Swansea. *Tom Moore*

Above: Although South Wales Transport ran a significant number of Bristol REs, the majority were acquired from other operators. Four coaches and 22 buses, all ECW-bodied, were inherited from United Welsh, while 20 Marshall-bodied RELL6Ls came from Western Welsh with the transfer of services in Neath and Haverfordwest. Of these latter, 15 had not yet entered service with their original owner, among them 636 (UKG 817J), seen near Pontardawe on 24 September 1983. *John Jones*

Left: The first municipal operator in South Wales to take the Bristol RE was Newport, which in 1967 placed in service eight ECW-bodied RESL6Ls. They did not pave the way for more, however, for, as at Leicester, subsequent saloons materialised as Metro-Scanias. Photographed while on hire to City of Cardiff Transport on 4 March 1976, No 107 (JDW 307F) shows off the brighter livery introduced in 1972. All of Newport's REs would be withdrawn in 1978. *C. Weller, courtesy Dave Thomas*

Below: Aberdare and its successor Cynon Valley took 13 ECW-bodied RESL6Ls in the years 1972/4/5. The 1974 batch included 13 (GHB 146N), seen at the garage at Gadlys on 25 August 1975. *John Jones*

Right: Merthyr Tydfil took four ECW-bodied RESL6Gs in 1973 but turned to East Lancs to body its 1974 quartet of RESL6Ls. No 202 (KDW 709P) is seen resplendent in Castle Street on 25 April 1984. *John Jones*

Right: Another South Wales municipality to favour the Bristol RE was Gelligaer. Three batches of three were ordered for the years 1972-4, the last batch being delivered to Rhymney Valley, into which Gelligaer had been pitched along with Caerphilly and tiny Bedwas & Machen following local-government reorganisation. Rhymney Valley 47 (NKG 247M), like all of them an ECW-bodied RESL6L, is pictured at Bargoed (Puzzle House) on 26 March 1982. *John Jones*

The Bristol RE was comparatively rare in Scotland, most examples being confined largely to long-distance coaching and thus just as likely to be found in England! In 1966 the Scottish Transport Group took delivery of an order for 65 RELH6Gs with Alexander Y-type bodywork — 45 for Scottish Omnibuses and 20 for Western SMT, most being fitted with toilets for services between London and Edinburgh or Glasgow. Western SMT T2184 (GAG 90D) was an additional vehicle, displayed (as T2179) at the 1966 Commercial Motor Show at Earl's Court. Seen here heading out of Glasgow for London on 10 July 1973, it would remain in the fleet until 1980. *Charles Dean / Author's collection*

Right: During the 1970s a number of Western SMT's Bristol RELH6G coaches passed to other Scottish Bus Group companies. Some were loaned to Alexander (Northern) and Alexander (Midland) for seasonal use, whilst two were sold to Highland; having had their toilets removed, this latter pair were re-seated from 38 up to 45 and fitted for one-man operation. Highland SL2 (DSD 701D), in full bus livery, stands in the rain at Inverness on 12 July 1973. In 1977 both vehicles would return to Western for further use. *Charles Dean / Author's collection*

Right: Scottish Omnibuses, trading as Eastern Scottish, also took Alexander Y-type-bodied Bristol RELH6Gs in 1966, to a total of 45. Five are seen here on layover at Hants & Dorset's Poole depot on 28 June 1975, having worked down to Bournemouth from Glasgow. Nearest the camera is XA162 (EWS 162D), numerically the first but amongst the second batch delivered, in March 1966. *John Jones*

The only RE buses new to a Scottish operator were 12 ECW-bodied RELL6Gs delivered to Alexander (Fife) in 1968 as FE21-32. (FE1-20, incidentally, were Bristol LS coaches of 1955.) Kirkcaldy-allocated FE24 (JXA 924F) is pictured in July 1974, the destination screen being the obvious departure from Tilling practice. All would remain in service until 1983 — a good innings for a non-standard type.
Charles Dean / Author's collection

Right: Later coaches for the Scottish Bus Group were 12m Bristol REMH6Gs with impressive Alexander M-type bodywork. Western SMT received 37 in 1969 and 1971, whilst Scottish Omnibuses took 33 in the years 1968-70. These latter ran originally in a striking livery of yellow and black, as shown on XA275 (LFS 275F) at the Dunbar Rally in August 1973. *Charles Dean / Author's collection*

Below: From 1976 the majority of the Scottish Bus Group's express coaches adopted a corporate livery of white and blue with 'SCOTTISH' fleetname and stylised St Andrew's cross. Among the vehicles so treated were the Bristol REMH6G/Alexander M types, represented here by Scottish Omnibuses XA372 (SFS 372H) heading north through Grantham on 26 June 1976. Scottish Omnibuses was to dispense with the services of its REMHs in 1982, although some of Western SMT's vehicles would soldier on until 1984.
Charles Dean / Author's collection

Although the Bristol RE was conceived as a workhorse for the Tilling Group it was Northern Ireland that ultimately saw the greatest concentration of the type. A batch of 20 RELL6Ls with Falkirk-built Alexander bodywork to Potter design, delivered to Ulsterbus in 1968 following the loan of RELL/ECW demonstrator LAE 770E, was followed by no fewer than 600 Alexander (Belfast)-bodied RELL6Gs for Ulsterbus/Citybus in the period 1975-83. Pictured at work in Londonderry on 23 March 1994 is Ulsterbus 2258 (ROI 2258), one of a batch of 40 delivered in 1978/9. *John Young*

Right: Buses in Northern Ireland inevitably became a target for terrorists and vandals during the troubled 1970s and '80s, and to combat these losses a considerable number of surplus vehicles was brought over from the mainland to provide a reserve fleet and a source of spares. Included were many Bristol REs, amongst the first to arrive, in 1980, being Citybus RELL6G/ECW 705 (SFM 22F), formerly Crosville SRG22, which survived to be photographed in Belfast on 16 June 1989. It would be withdrawn as time-expired (rather than battle-damaged) a couple of months later. *John Young*

Right: Just three Bristol REs — all Plaxton-bodied RELH6Ls — were bought new by operators in the Irish Republic. Two were coaches, but the third, supplied in August 1969 to Doyle, Roundwood, trading as St Kevin's Bus Service, was fitted with a Derwent bus body seating 55. Seen on its operator's Dublin–Glendalough service, with an ex-Ribble Saro-bodied Leyland Tiger Cub behind, ONI 300 would later pass to Merseyside independent Davies of Halewood, being re-registered GEM 884N. *Mike Sutcliffe*

Left: The only other export market for the Bristol RE was New Zealand, the Christchurch Transport Board being the recipient of 152 RELL6Ls produced between 1974 and 1981. Bodywork was built locally under licence, initially by Hawke to ECW design and later by New Zealand Motor Bodies to a design by Swiss builder Hess. Representing the former is 481 (HO 4672), from the earliest batch, delivered in 1974/5; note the row of hooks under the windscreen, used for carrying folded pushchairs. *Author's collection*

Left: In 1990 the Christchurch Transport Board was succeeded by a new company, Redbus, and the resulting loss of services to tender saw the first withdrawals of REs. These were subsequently dispersed throughout New Zealand, and at the time of writing the largest collection of survivors is to be found on the North Island, with Bayline Coachlines, of Tauranga, where they are used on schools duties. Dating from 1978 and formerly CTB 518, NZMB/Hess-bodied 47 (JD 3227) was photographed leaving the depot in March 2007. *Martin Curtis*